Contents

This is our kitchen.

We cook most food on the hob
and bake cakes and pies
in the electric oven.

Dirty dishes are washed
in the dishwasher.

4

Cooking

Ruth Thomson

Note for parents and teachers

The Changing Times series is soundly based on the requirements of the History Curriculum. Using the device of four generations of a real family, the author combines reminiscences of this family with other people's oral evidence. The oral history is matched with photographs and other contemporary sources. Many other lessons are hidden in the text, which practises the skills of chronological sequencing, gives reference to a timeline and introduces the language and vocabulary of the past. Young children will find much useful information here, as well as a new understanding of the recent history of everyday situations and familiar things.

This edition 2004

Franklin Watts
96 Leonard Street
London EC2A 4XD

Franklin Watts Australia
45–51 Huntley Street
Alexandria
NSW 2015

Copyright © 1992 Franklin Watts

Editor: Sarah Ridley
Designer: Michael Leaman
Educational consultant: John West
Photographer: Peter Millard

A CIP catalogue record for this book is available from the British Library.
Dewey Decimal Classification Number: 641.5
ISBN 0 7496 5249 7

Acknowledgements: The author and publishers would like to thank the following people and organisations for their help with the preparation of this book: Lisa Chaney; Jessie Baker, Jessie Ridley and Suzanne Ridley; Kim Sinclair of Kitchen and Country Antiques and Diana Green for the loan of items from their collections.

Printed in Malaysia

We keep milk, butter, eggs
and other foods that need
to keep cool in the fridge,
and frozen foods in the freezer.

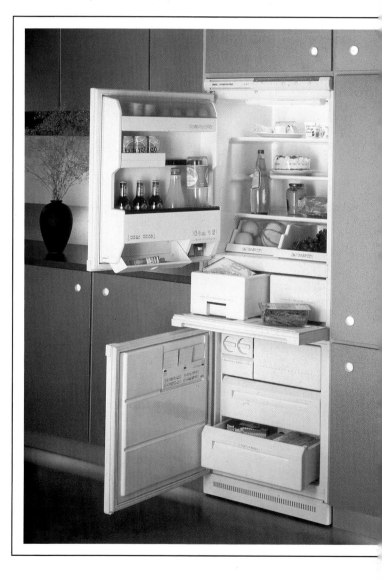

Sometimes Mum uses
the microwave to cook
quick meals.

We make toast in the toaster for breakfast.

We boil water in the jug kettle for tea and coffee.

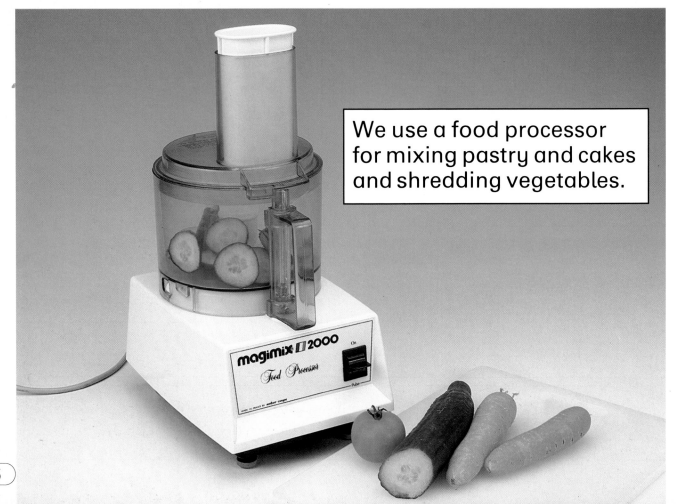

We use a food processor for mixing pastry and cakes and shredding vegetables.

These are some of our cooking utensils.

Bread knife

Egg whisk

Grater

Sieve

Spatula

Kitchen knife

Slice

Ice-cream scoop

Tin opener

Measuring jug

Rolling pin

Lemon squeezer

Corkscrew

Wooden spoons

I asked Mum what her kitchen was like when she was young.

She said,

'We cooked on a gas stove. It had a plate rack and a grill pan.'

'The kettle was heated on the stove. It whistled when the water boiled.'

'A geyser heated the water.
The gas made
a loud popping noise
when it came on.'

'Milk, eggs and meat
were kept cool
in a meat safe.'

When Mum's family moved house,
they had a new kitchen with fitted units.

Mum said,

'There was such excitement when we got a fridge.
It was taller than I was.'

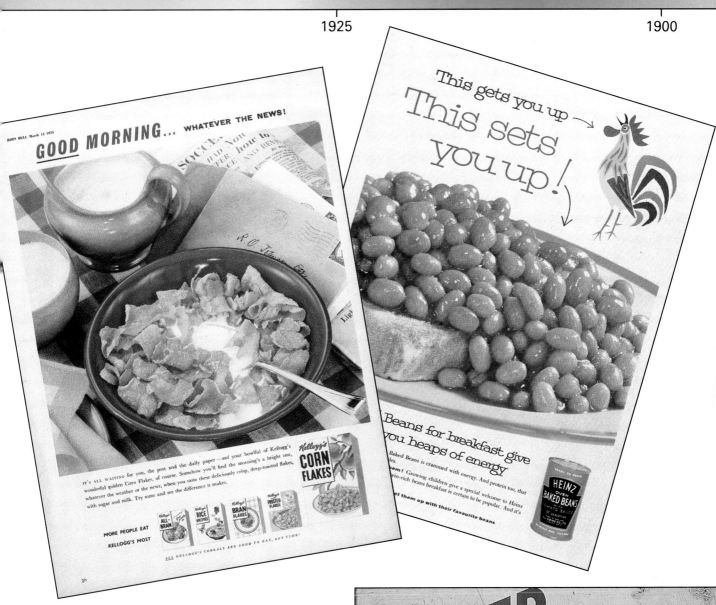

'For breakfast, we ate
cereals and toast.
On Sundays, there was
cooked breakfast.
I liked beans on toast.'

'My favourite drinks were
Tizer, Peardrax and lemonade.'

I asked Granny about the kitchen
her family had when she was young.

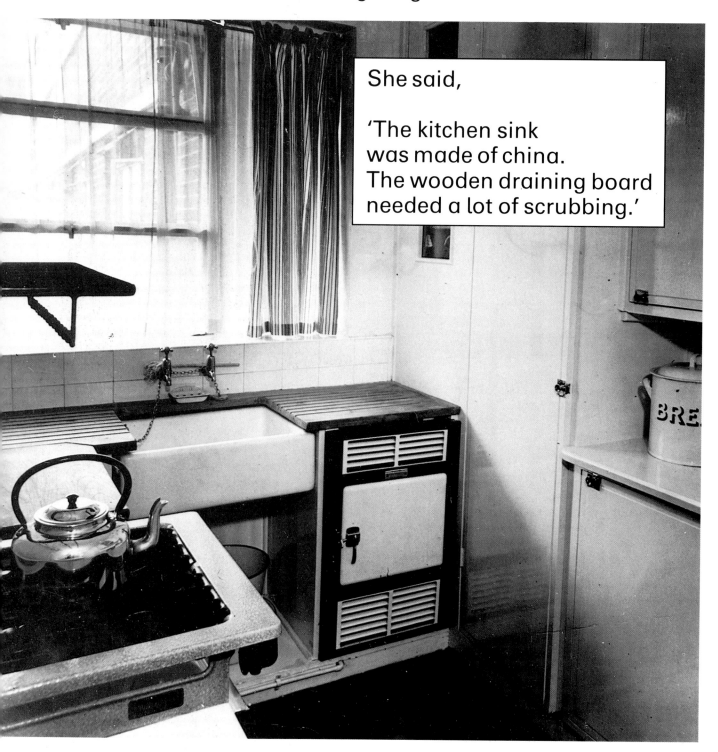

She said,

'The kitchen sink
was made of china.
The wooden draining board
needed a lot of scrubbing.'

12

'We had a gas cooker on legs. It had a grill for making toast.'

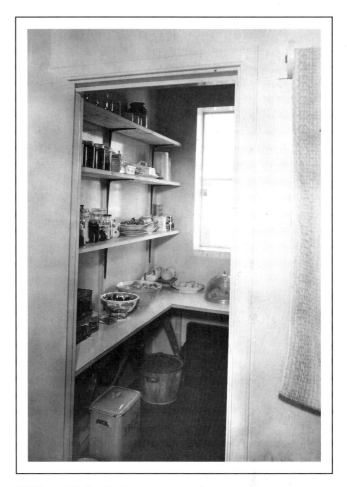

'We didn't have a fridge. Food was kept cold in the larder. It had red floor tiles.'

'Some families had a fridge. They were quite expensive.'

Granny now

1975　　　　　　　　　　195

Granny said,

'We ate bread and jam for breakfast,
stews or sausages for lunch
and sandwiches or toast at teatime.'

1930s toaster

Who spotted SPOTTED DICK?

McDougall's
the SELF-RAISING FLOUR that never varies

'My favourite
dishes were
puddings.'

'Once a week, a mincer was clamped
to the side of the table.
Leftovers from the Sunday roast
were minced to make pasties
or shepherd's pie.'

'Some of our neighbours
used a kitchen range
to cook on.
Others had Agas
or electric ovens.'

1975   195●

Granny told me that her mother spent a lot of time in the kitchen.

She said,

'My mother made all her own scones, and teacakes for teatime.'

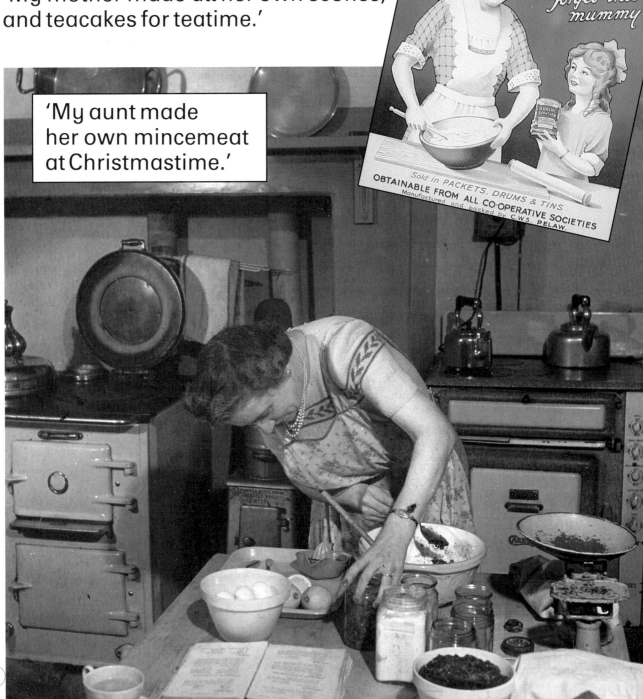

'My aunt made her own mincemeat at Christmastime.'

C·W·S BAKING POWDER

"You mustn't forget this mummy"

Sold in PACKETS, DRUMS & TINS
OBTAINABLE FROM ALL CO-OPERATIVE SOCIETIES
Manufactured and packed by C.W.S. PELAW.

'In January, she made enough marmalade to last us the rest of the year.'

TRANSPARENT
CRYSTAL
JAM POT COVERS

3D

TRANSPARENT CIRCLES
WAXED CIRCLES
RUBBER BANDS
GUMMED LABELS
and Tested Recipes
for Jam Making.

1 lb. size

'In summertime, she made jams and jellies with gooseberries, redcurrants and cherries.'

When the Second World War came, some foods became very scarce.

Granny said,

'Everyone had a ration book to take shopping with them.'

'You could only buy small amounts of butter, cheese and meat each, so there was enough for all.'

'The government issued cookery leaflets to show people how to make best use of their food.'

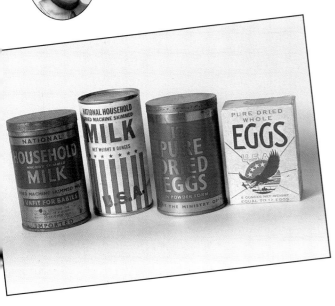

'I remember we used dried egg from a packet and dried milk from a tin. The taste was all right once you got used to it.'

'Sometimes our friends ate at a wartime kitchen, especially if their parents were busy with war work.'

Great-granny told me there was no electricity
at all in her house when she was young.
There wasn't a fridge or an electric cooker.

She said,

'Food was cooked on a coal-fired range.
Saucepans were put on top.
Pies were cooked in the oven.
Rubbish was burned in the fire.'

'A cast-iron kettle was kept hot on top of the stove all day long.'

'Bread was toasted on a toasting fork in front of the fire.'

'Knives used to rust, because they were made of steel. We didn't have stainless steel then. One of my jobs was to clean and polish them on a knifeboard.'

1975   1950

I asked Great-granny
where food was kept.

She said,

'Fresh food
was kept in the larder.
It had a stone floor
and a marble shelf to
help keep things cool.'

'Bread was kept
in an enormous
earthenware crock.
The bread board
was its lid.'

'The milk jug stood in a bowl of cold water to stop the milk from going off.
A muslin cloth on top kept flies out.'

'Meat was kept under a gauze meat cover so flies and mice couldn't get at it.'

'Cheese was kept in a covered cheese dish or in a cheese cloth in the larder.'

23

1975   1950

Great-granny said,

'We had the same meals
every day of every week.'

'Roast on a Sunday.
Cold leftovers on a Monday
which was busy washday.
Meat pie on a Tuesday.
Meat stew on Wednesday.
Meat pudding on Thursday
Sausages on Friday.
Saturday was whatever
Mother felt like —
rabbit was a favourite.'

'At bedtime, we drank cocoa
and ate toast and dripping.'

'Friday was baking day.
My mother baked cakes, biscuits and pies.
The house smelt warm and welcoming.'

1975   1950

These are some of the kitchen utensils
that Great-granny had when she was young.
They are all made of metal, wood or pottery.

Potato
masher

Mortar and pestle
(for grinding up spices)

Colander

Sugar
nippers

Pudding
mould

Knives

Pattypan

Can opener

Corkscrew

Vegetable
chopper

Spoon

Biscuit
cutters

Which ones have you never seen before?
Compare these utensils with those on page 7.
Have any of them changed shape or material?

Grater

Storage jar

Coffee grinder

Gravy strainer

Spice box

Jelly mould

Nutmeg grater

Whisks

Things to do

Which of these objects
do you have in your kitchen?
Which ones do you think your parents,
grandparents or great-grandparents had?
Look back through the book to help you.

Do you ever have take-away meals?

Ask some grown-ups what take-away meals
they had when they were young.

This is what Great-granny's kitchen was like. What is the same about it as your kitchen? What is different?

Index

Photographs: Advertising Archives 10, 11(tl), 11(tr); Barnaby's cover (bl), 8(b), 13(tr), 17(t); Beamish title page (t), 23(t), 23(c); © British Gas plc endpapers, 8(t); Cadbury Ltd 24(b); Lisa Chaney 22(tr), 31; © Coggs Manor Farm Museum cover (tl), 20; Mary Evans Picture Library 14(br); Chris Fairclough 4(br), 5(bl), 6(b); Sally and Richard Greenhill 4(l); Hulton Picture Company cover (tr), 12, 14(t), 24(t), 30(tr); with thanks to the Trustees of the Imperial War Museum 19(b); Magnet plc cover (br), title page (b), 4-5(t); thanks to McDonald's 30(b); Peter Millard imprint page, 6(tl), 6(tr), 7, 9(b), 14(bl), 15(t), 21(all), 22(b), 23(b), 25, 26-27, 28, 29(c), 29(bl), 29(br); Moulinex Swan Holdings 29(t); Museum of East Anglian Life 18(bl), 18(br); Robert Opie 11(b), 13(br), 16(t), 18(t), 19(t); Topham Picture Source 15(b), 16(b), 30(tl); thanks to Zanussi Ltd 5(tr), 13(l).